BASEBALL

Written by

Kay Robertson

rourkeeducationalmedia.com

Scan for Related Titles
and Teacher Resources

© 2014 Rourke Educational Media

All rights reserved. No part of this book may be reproduced or utilized in any form or by any means, electronic or mechanical including photocopying, recording, or by any information storage and retrieval system without permission in writing from the publisher.

www.rourkeeducationalmedia.com

PHOTO CREDITS: Cover: © ; Title Page: © Michael Ciu; Page 4: © Lawrence Weslowski Jr.; Page 5: © kali9; Page 6: © Brian McEntire; Page 7: © Glenn Nagel; Page 8: © Nicholas Piccillo; Page 9: © Monkey Business Images; Page 10: © Aspen Photo; Page 11: © ranplett; Page 12: © Photographerlondon; Page 13: © Tony Tremblay; Page 14: © 4x6; Page 15: © james boulette; Page 16: © Cynthia Farmer; Page 17: © George Peters; Page 18: © Ben Conlan; Page 19: © tammykayphoto; Page 20: © Dallas John; Page 21: © Michael Ciu; Page 22: © Jeff Williams;

Editor: Precious McKenzie

Cover and Interior Designer: Tara Raymo

Library of Congress PCN Data

Baseball / Kay Robertson
Fun Sports for Fitness
ISBN 978-1-62169-853-1 (hardcover)
ISBN 978-1-62169-748-0 (softcover)
ISBN 978-1-62169-955-2 (e-Book)
Library of Congress Control Number: 2013936458

Rourke Educational Media
Printed in the United States of America,
North Mankato, Minnesota

Rourke Educational Media

rourkeeducationalmedia.com

customerservice@rourkeeducationalmedia.com • PO Box 643328 Vero Beach, Florida 32964

Table of Contents

America's Favorite Sport 4

The Pitcher: A Key Player 6

Ready, Set, SWING! 8

Catcher: Boss on the Field 12

Fielding the Ball 14

Running the Bases 18

Umpiring a Game 22

Glossary 23

Show What You Know 24

America's Favorite Sport

Baseball is more than just a popular sport for boys and girls. Although it's part of the fabric of America, its popularity is worldwide.

A baseball field, or **diamond**, consists of the infield and the outfield. The diamond is formed by the placement of bases, including home plate. The object of the game is to put players on bases and score runs by crossing home plate.

The baseball diamond is formed by the baselines. At the center of the infield is the pitcher's mound; beyond the infield is the outfield grass.

Baseball is the only game in which the **offensive** team—the team "at bat"—can't touch the ball. If a batter or baserunner does touch the ball, he or she will be ruled out.

While organized baseball is played mostly by boys, there are no rules that say girls can't join in the fun. In fact, any girl who wants to test her baseball skills playing with and against boys is welcome to try out.

Many girls play softball in the United States. Softball is similar to baseball except for the size of the ball, the distance between bases, and the pitching style. Many people love to play baseball and softball.

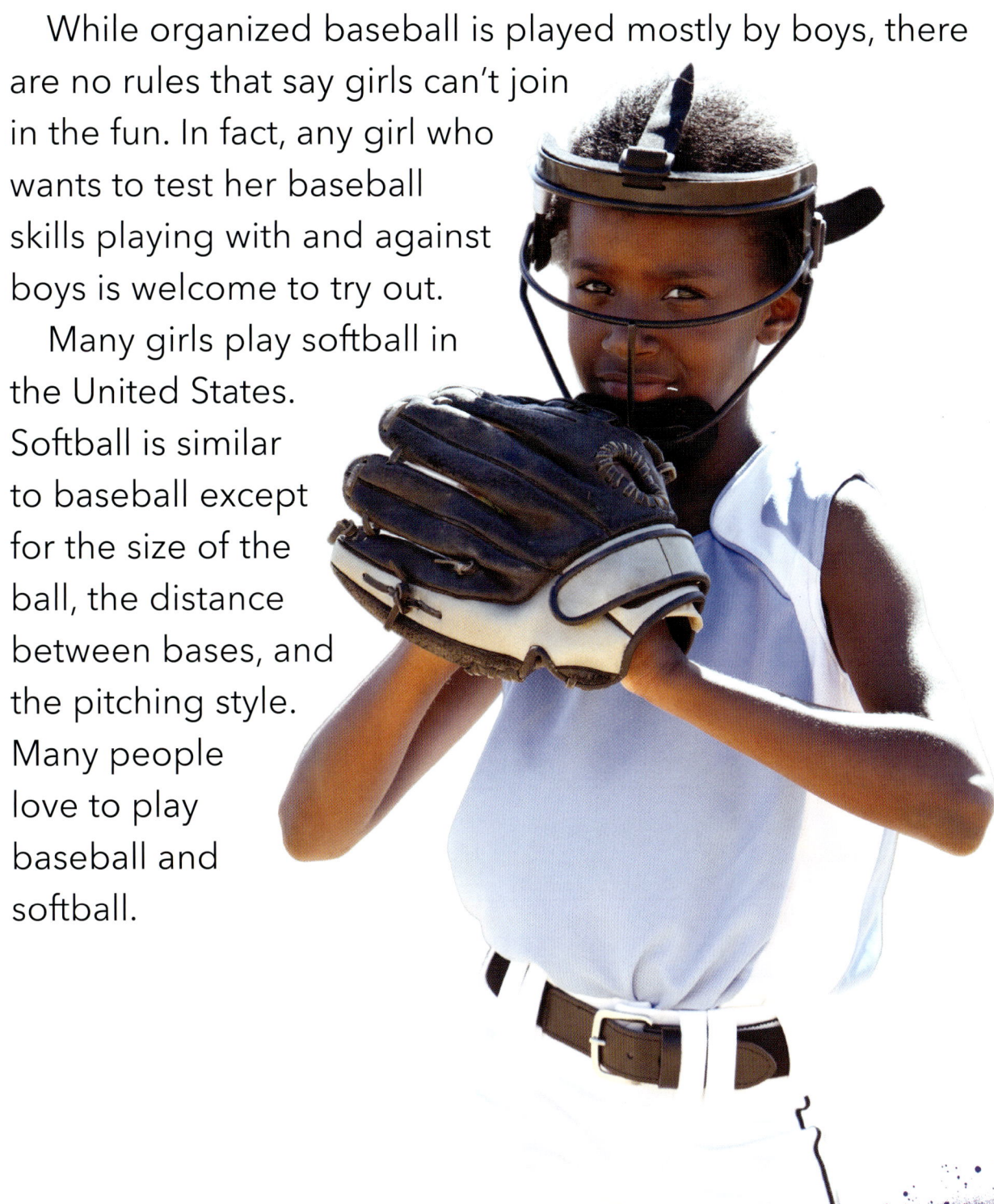

The Pitcher: A Key Player

The strike zone is an invisible rectangular box the width of home plate. It extends from the batter's knees to the letters on the front of his uniform.

The key player on the **defensive** team, the team on the field, is the pitcher. Standing on a slightly **elevated** mound, the pitcher puts the ball into play and tries to keep the opponent from hitting the ball. Pitches are called strikes or balls by the **umpire**, depending on whether they are in the strike zone.

Pitchers grip the ball with and against the seams to change the way the ball moves. A curve ball approaches the batter in an arcing path with slightly less pace. A fastball comes more directly and with more **velocity**. A change-up looks like a fastball in the delivery, but travels more slowly.

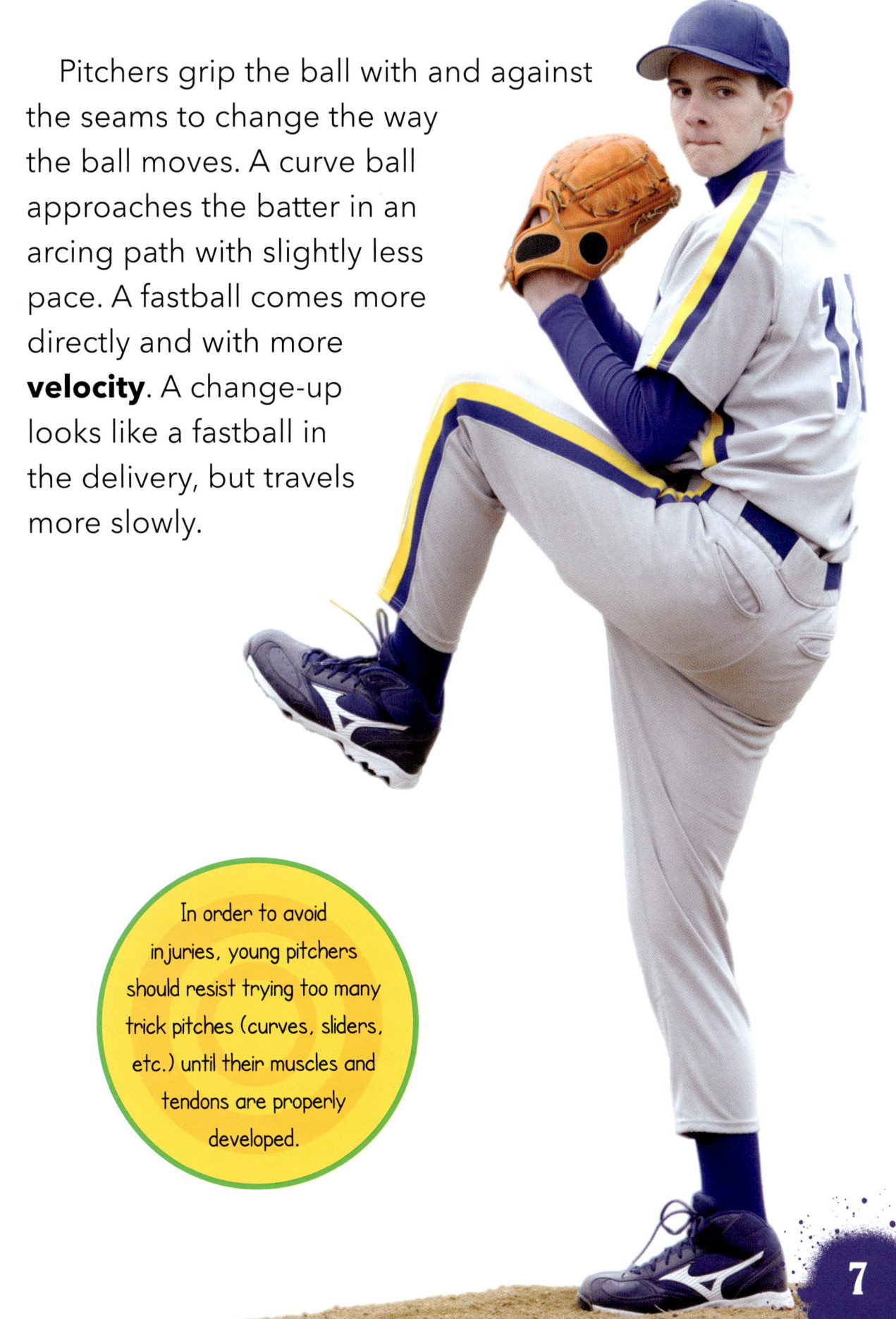

In order to avoid injuries, young pitchers should resist trying too many trick pitches (curves, sliders, etc.) until their muscles and tendons are properly developed.

Ready, Set, SWING!

Batting is an **essential** part of the game. Few skills are as hard as hitting one round object, the ball, with another rounded surface, the bat. The first rule is to keep your eyes on the ball from the moment it leaves the pitcher's hand until it makes contact with your bat.

There are three major parts to a good swing. They are the stride, the swing, and the follow-through. As you swing, shift your weight forward. Keep your hands high and bring the bat around, driving through the ball. After making contact, keep your head still and finish the swing.

Your hands should be together on the handle of the bat. Hold the bat firmly, but try to relax. When you bring the bat around, keep the elbow of your bottom hand tucked close to your body. Your arms and hands should form a "V" as you make contact.

The follow-through is very important. It finishes the swing and **ensures** all your energy and power have been fully delivered through the bat to the ball. If you chop at the pitch and don't follow through, you won't be able to generate maximum power.

When swinging the bat, the golden rule is to keep your head still. With a pitch coming at you hard and fast, your focus can mean the difference between a base hit and a strike-out.

When picking a bat, choose carefully. Experiment during practice to see what works best. The most important factors are comfort and bat speed. You can hit the ball farther using a light bat and quick hands than you will with a heavy bat you can't swing.

Catcher: Boss on the Field

Even though the pitcher is often the star of the team, the catcher is the boss on the field. In organized games, the catcher calls the pitches, which means signaling the pitcher to throw a curve ball or a strike. The catcher must be a good, strong, durable athlete.

For protection, catchers wear a variety of equipment. This includes a helmet and face mask. Also, the catcher straps on shin guards and a thick chest pad to protect against foul balls.

Ironically, the gear a catcher wears is called "the tools of ignorance" because catching is a thankless job. But the catcher is usually a very smart player who knows the game very well.

Because of **aluminum** bats, catchers don't have to worry about being struck by broken bats. However, they do have to worry about being run over by baserunners trying to score at home plate.

The catcher and the home plate umpire spend the whole game together.

13

Fielding the Ball

In addition to the pitcher and catcher, there are seven defensive positions. They are first, second, and third base, shortstop, who is positioned between second and third base, and the three outfielders: left, right, and center field. Infielders must always be ready, have their knees bent, gloves open, and their eyes on the ball.

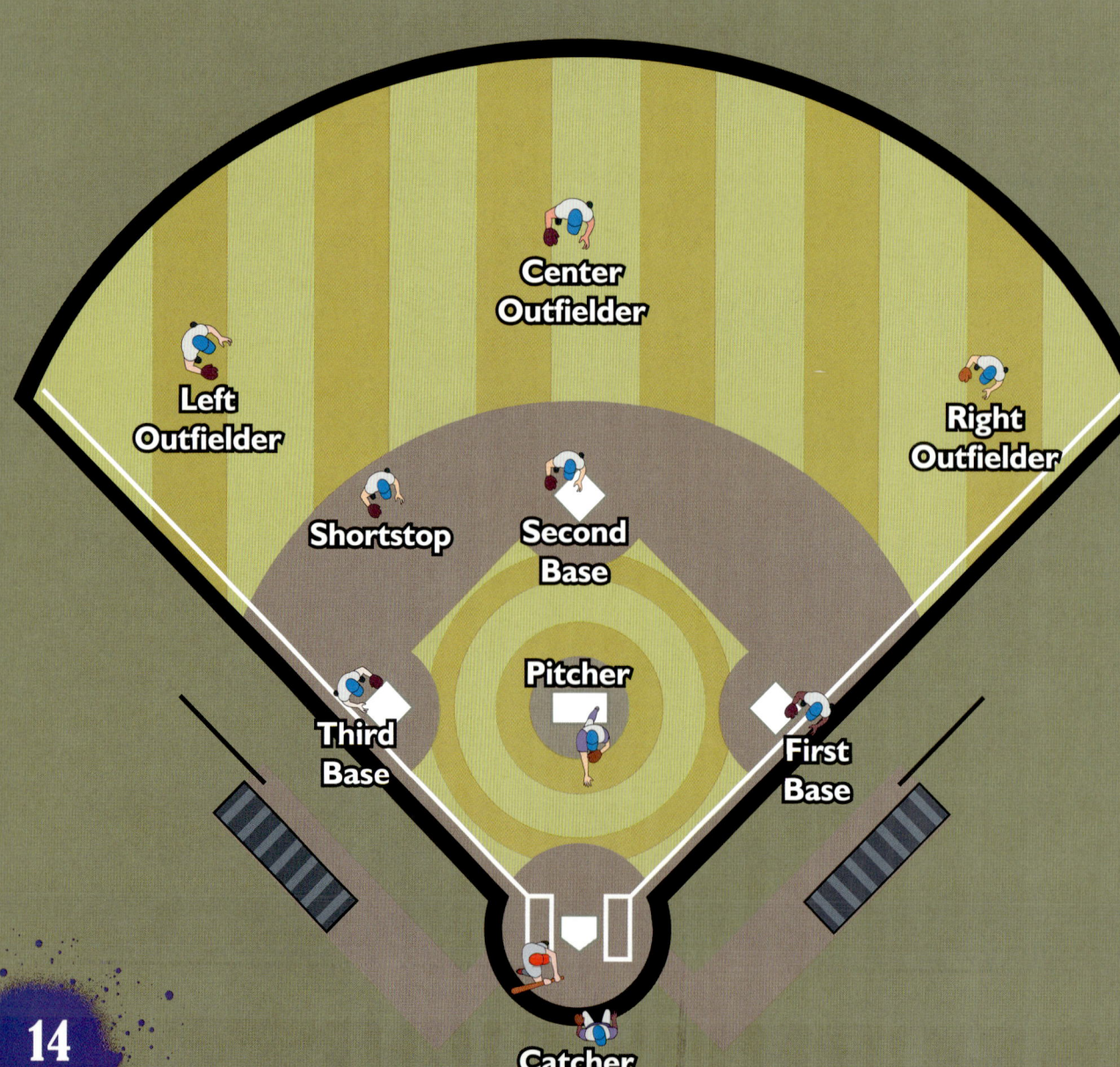

A good infielder is always alert, watching the batter and any baserunners.

The first baseman's mitt is different than other infielders' gloves. It has a flat side and looks like a crab claw. The flat side helps the fielder catch throws in the dirt.

To catch an infield grounder correctly, let the ball roll into your outstretched glove, then trap it with your throwing hand. Outfielders taking fly balls should hold their glove high and keep their throwing hand near the mitt. If you bobble the ball, you may have a second chance to trap it.

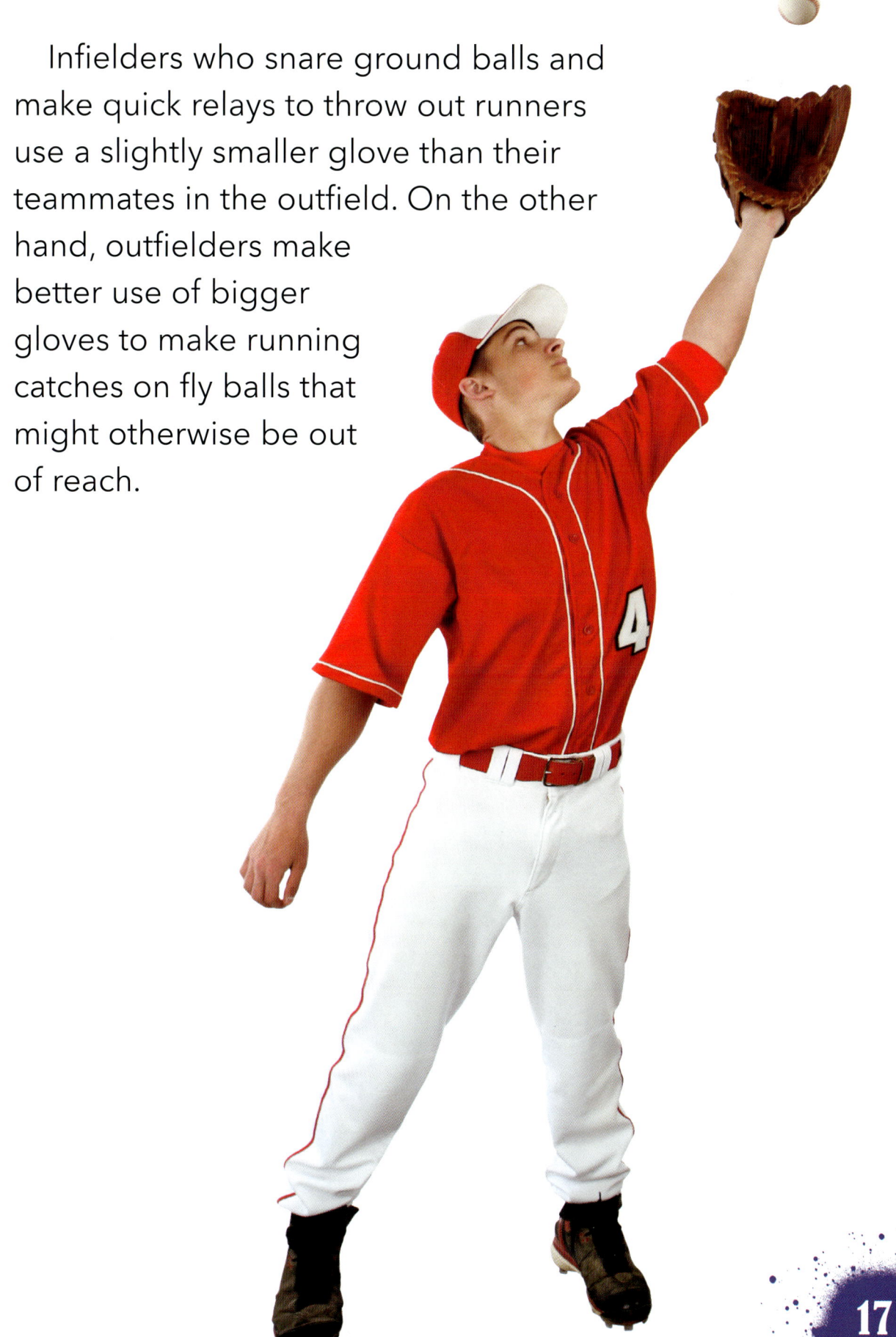

Infielders who snare ground balls and make quick relays to throw out runners use a slightly smaller glove than their teammates in the outfield. On the other hand, outfielders make better use of bigger gloves to make running catches on fly balls that might otherwise be out of reach.

Running the Bases

Another important element of baseball is baserunning. A batter becomes a baserunner the moment contact is made with the ball. On a ground ball to one of the infielders, the batter must sprint to first base. If he beats the relay from the infielder, the runner earns an infield hit.

If a batted ball clears the infield, the batter should run to first base while watching to see how the ball is played by the outfielder. The runner may round first base and head toward second base. If the ball is fielded cleanly, the runner retreats to first base. If not, the runner may advance.

First base is the only base a runner may overrun to beat a throw from one of the infielders. If the runner rounds the base, however, he or she may be tagged out.

Baserunners can be caught off base if they're not careful. If a runner on first base doesn't reach second base before a relay, he is forced out. If he runs on a fly ball and can't get back after the putout is made and before the ball is relayed to the fielder at that base, he's out.

Baserunners may lead-off a base. This means taking a couple of steps toward the next base. But a runner can only do so once the pitcher has delivered. If the ball gets away from the catcher, the runner may attempt to advance. This is called stealing.

One of the most exciting plays is when a baserunner is caught between bases, and the defensive team has to chase him down and tag him out.

Umpiring a Game

Most youth baseball games call for two umpires, or referees, on the field. One stands behind home plate and wears a mask and chest protector like the catcher. His job is to call balls and strikes. His partner stands near second base and makes the calls on infield plays at the bases. Together they ensure that this exciting game is fairly played by both sides.

Glossary

aluminum (ah-LOO-muh-num): a silvery-white metallic element

defensive (di-FEN-siv): the team that tries to prevent runs from being scored

diamond (DYE-mond): the playing field in a game of baseball or softball

elevated (EL-uh-vayt-ed): raised above a given level

ensures (en-SHOORZ): to make positive

essential (ee-SEN-chul): something that is necessary; basic

offensive (uh-FEN-siv): the team trying to score runs; the team at bat

umpire (UHM-pie-er): a referee or judge hired to rule on plays

velocity (vuh-LOS-it-ee): rate of speed

Index

baserunning   18
batting   8-11
catcher(s)   12, 13, 14, 21, 22
change-up   7
curve ball   7, 12
diamond   4
fastball   7
fielding   14-17
fly ball(s)   16, 17, 20
follow-through   8, 10
gloves (for fielding)   14, 16, 17
ground ball(s)   17, 18
home plate   4, 6, 13, 22
pitcher(s)   4, 6, 7, 8, 12, 14, 21
shortstop   14
stride   8
strike zone   6
strike-out   11
swing   8, 10, 11
umpire(s)   6, 13, 22

Websites to Visit

mlb.mlb.com/mlb/kids/index.jsp

gws.ala.org/tags/baseball

pleasanthillbaberuth.com/players-area/baseball-sites-for-kids

Show What You Know

1. Why is a first basemen's glove different from other infielders' gloves?
2. How many bases are there on a baseball field?
3. When hitting the ball, why is it important to keep your head still?
4. By looking at the pictures in the book, who do you think wears the most equipment?
5. Who is the key player on the defensive team?